Editor: Roger Vlitos
Editorial planning: Clark Robinson Ltd
Design: David West
Children's Book Design
Illustrator: Aziz Khan
Picture research: Cecilia Weston-Baker

Photographic Credits:
Vanessa Bailey; pages 4/5, page 7 (left & right), page 10 (top), page 11 (top), page 12 (bottom), page 18 (top), page 24 (bottom). Roger Vlitos: page 7 (bottom), page 9 (top-left), page 10 (bottom), page 13 (bottom), page 17 (top & bottom), page 20 (bottom), page 21 (top), page 22 (bottom), page 23 (top & bottom), page 25 (left & right), page 26 (bottom), page 27 (bottom), page 28 (bottom), page 29 (centre), page 30 (top). Shaun Barlow: page 14 (top & bottom), page 16 (bottom), page 29 (bottom), page 30 (bottom). Mary Evans Picture Library: page 11 (bottom), page 13 (top).

© Aladdin Books Ltd
70 Old Compton Street
London W1

*First published in Great Britain
in 1989 by*
Gloucester Press
96 Leonard Street
London EC2A 4RH

ISBN 0-7496-0048-9

All rights reserved

Printed in Belgium

The publishers wish to point out that all photos appearing in this book were either loaned by an agency or shot with posed models.

Some of the subject areas covered by this book fall outside the area of expertise of the author, Harry Shapiro. The information for these sections has been provided by experts through Clark Robinson Limited.

Facts on
Inhalants

Harry Shapiro

GLOUCESTER PRESS
London · New York · Toronto · Sydney

CONTENTS

WHAT ARE
INHALANTS?
6

WHICH ARE
SNIFFED?
8

MEDICAL
INHALANTS
12

WHY DO
PEOPLE SNIFF?
16

WHAT IS THE
EFFECT?
20

IMMEDIATE
DANGERS
24

LONG-TERM
DANGERS
26

INHALANTS
IN SOCIETY
28

THE LAW
30

GLOSSARY & INDEX
31   32

INTRODUCTION 5

Sniffing something to change the way you feel has a long history. One hundred years ago rich people at parties used to sniff a liquid called ether. But solvent sniffing among ordinary young people started only about 20 years ago. There are many substances that can be sniffed. Most young people who do it are between 12 and 18 years old. They may do it only a few times and come to no harm. But, some carry on for months or years. A very few unlucky ones die the first time they try it. This book will give you all the facts about inhalants -why people sniff, the effects, the dangers and the law. You will also find some addresses on the back pages. These will help you if you want some more information or you want help for yourself or a friend.

This is just a sample of the many products that are sometimes sniffed. They include – glues, paint, sprays, nail varnish, petrol, lighter fuel – even fire extinguishers!

6 WHAT ARE INHALANTS?

Most inhalants are solvents. They are sometimes also called volatile hydrocarbons. They belong to the hydrogen and carbon families of chemicals. Many are made mainly from coal and products of the chemical industry. Others, however, are made from vegetables which have rotted down. There are two special things about all of the solvents which are sniffed. First, they must give off a strong vapour. Second, the vapour that they give off makes you feel very different from the way you feel normally. Inhaling, or breathing in, these gases can often make people feel sick. However, some people enjoy the way it makes them dizzy, delirious or energetic. Many inhalants are harmful to the human body. Most can damage your health if you are careless.

How they work

Industry finds solvents very useful. Without solvents, many products like glue and paint would harden before you came to use them. The job of a solvent is to keep the product dissolved in the container until it is ready for use. Then the product is either spread (like glue) or poured (like petrol) or squirted (like hair spray). Once that happens, the solvent disperses quickly into the air. When doors and windows are kept shut in a room where solvents have been used we are in danger of inhaling them.

Solvent keeps the product liquid and makes it easy to apply

Solvent evaporates quickly, leaving a thin layer of product to dry

Glues

Many glues consist of a substance such as rubber or a plastic dissolved in a solvent that evaporates easily. Model-making glue is usually of this kind. However, some model-makers use neat solvent. This can give off very powerful vapours.

Sprays

Aerosols containing solvents include deodorants, paints and lacquers. The propellant, the gas that pushes the substance out of the can, may also be inhaled. People often wear masks to protect them from harmful side-effects.

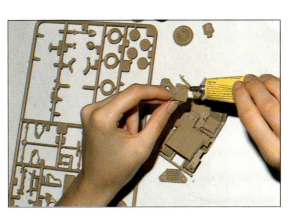

Paints

There are many kinds of paints, but all of them, except for water-based "emulsion" paints, contain a solvent or "vehicle" that evaporates as the paint dries. The most volatile (that is, the most easily evaporated) solvents are in quick-drying paints such as cellulose lacquers. But ordinary oil-based paints and varnishes also give off harmful fumes, both while they are in the can and when they are drying. For this reason, professional painters often wear face masks while they work.

8 WHICH ARE SNIFFED?

An inhalant is anything that gives off vapours or fumes that can be breathed deep into the lungs. There are hundreds of such substances at home, or in shops and workplaces. Common ones are glues, aerosols and paints. Others include cigarette lighter fuel – both liquid and gas, dry cleaning fluid, nail varnish, petrol, camping gas, fire extinguisher fluid, paint thinners, and even typewriter correction fluid. The list is almost endless. Most of these substances can be bought in a supermarket or "do-it-yourself" shop. Most contain chemicals called solvents; and many other solvents are used in industry, particularly for cleaning away oil and grease. For the most part people inhale solvents accidentally. There are guidelines to protect health in the factories where inhalants are used.

Solvents in industry

In an electroplating works, large tanks of solvents are used to "de-grease" metal articles before they are plated. The fumes from the tanks are regarded as a hazard for the workers, and special fans and ventilators are normally provided. Nevertheless, sometimes a worker becomes addicted to breathing in the solvent, and some have even been killed doing so. To avoid health hazards, most workers wear masks.

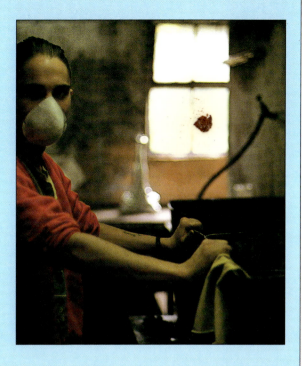

How many in the shops?

Many different kinds of inhalants can be bought in shops, particularly those that sell paints and varnishes, adhesives or cleaning agents. Many paints, together with the solvents used to thin them and the solutions for removing them, contain inhalants. Paints in aerosol cans may contain both solvents and propellant gases that can be inhaled. Adhesives include solvent-type glues, such as those used for sticking paper and plastics, and resin-type adhesives designed to glue wood and metal. The glues themselves give off inhalant fumes, and so do articles stuck with them as the glue is drying. Cleaning agents sold for removing grease and stains from clothing or carpets usually consist of solvents. These are very dangerous inhalants and some people have been overcome by their fumes.

10 WHICH ARE SNIFFED?

In the office

Common inhalants in offices include solutions for removing stencil ink, typewriter correction fluid and the solvent used for "thinning" it. In a drawing office, artists and draughtsmen may use aerosols containing adhesives and fixatives for spraying drawings.

In the garage

Most cars run on petrol, and this substance is the commonest inhalant in a garage. Many people keep a spare can of petrol, either for the car or perhaps for a lawn-mower. Some people also keep paraffin (kerosene) in their garages, along with paint and paint thinners. Aerosols may contain special substances for damp-proofing a car's electrical system or spraying into the engine to help it start in cold weather.

Around the home

Inhalants can be found in various places in the home, from the kitchen to the bedroom. Many cleaning fluids and polishes, such as liquids, "squeezy" bottles, pump-sprays and aerosols, are solvent-based and therefore potential inhalants. Aerosol deodorants and perfume sprays contain inhalable solvents and propellant gases. Nail varnish, and the solvent used to remove it, are also inhalants. Even benzene, the fluid used by stamp collectors to reveal watermarks in stamps, is a dangerous inhalant. Many stamp collectors now wear special face-masks to avoid inhaling the poisonous benzene fumes.

19th-century inhalers

Two of the earliest anaesthetics, substances used to make a patient unconscious during a surgical operation, were nitrous oxide gas and ether vapour. Nitrous oxide was also known as "laughing gas" because inhaling it makes people feel very happy. Some people even held "laughing gas" parties.

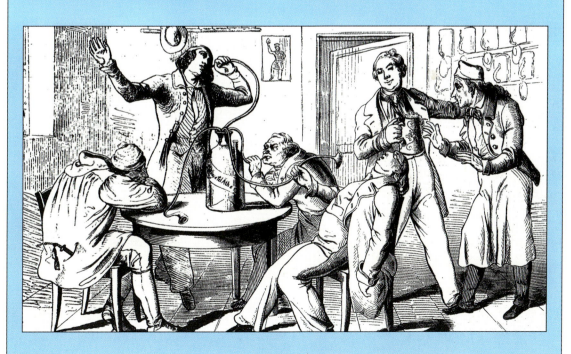

12 MEDICAL INHALANTS

Doctors administer medicinal drugs in two main ways, either as tablets or injections. A few medicines are given as inhalants, particularly drugs for treating disorders of the body's airways: the nose, throat, windpipe and lungs. Inhalants are easy to give and act almost at once. Much smaller amounts are needed than if the drugs were swallowed or injected. A spray breaks the solution containing the medicine into tiny droplets, which are blown into the mouth or nose and inhaled at the same time. Many inhalants are supplied in small aerosols, which use a gas to propel the spray. A "rotahaler" has a small fan which mixes a finely powdered medicine with air, so that it can be inhaled. The main problem with many of these inhalants is that they can have side-effects on the body.

Into the lungs

Asthma narrows the body's fine airways leading to the lungs by causing a spasm in the tiny muscles in their walls and difficulty in breathing. This may result from an infection, a nervous upset or an allergy.

Medical sprays and inhalants are called bronchodilators. They work by relaxing, or widening, the contracted muscles and so letting air through to the lungs. Many asthma sufferers find that they cannot lead a normal life without these inhalants.

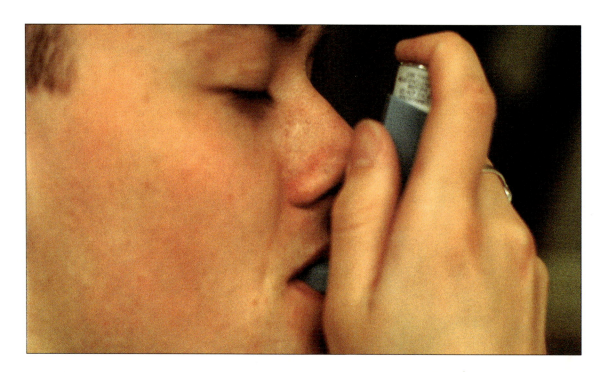

Reviving the unconscious

An old remedy to "bring round" somebody who had fainted was to let them either inhale the fumes of burnt feathers or smelling salts. The fumes contained ammonia. Today, the vapour of amyl nitrate, carried in breakable capsules, is inhaled by people with the heart condition called angina.

Oxygen

Oxygen from the air is needed by the body to help provide energy. Without it tissues rapidly die. It is transferred from our breath to the tissues through the lungs and bloodstream. When these are damaged, as in severe bronchitis and heart disease, an enriched supply can be provided by a portable cylinder and face mask. Most ambulances carry these.

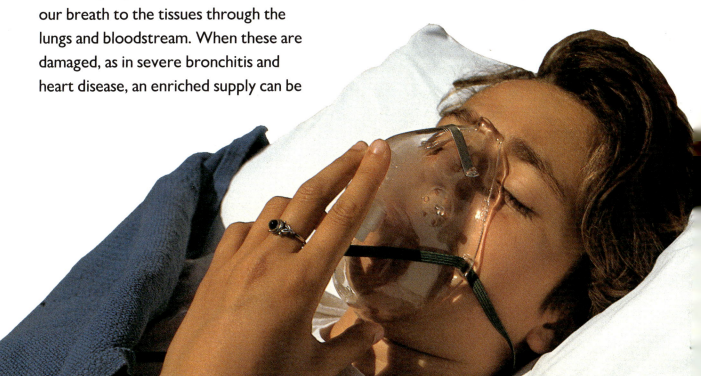

14 MEDICAL INHALANTS

For hay fever

Every year during summer, particularly in fine weather, pollen carried in the air irritates the airways of allergic people. They have a runny nose and watering eyes, just as if they had a cold. These symptoms of hay fever can be treated with nasal sprays and inhalers, which deliver drugs to the membranes lining the nose. They contain antihistamines, which lessen the allergic reaction. Sometimes hay fever affects the finer tubes in the lungs and causes symptoms identical to asthma. These can include breathlessness which can be severe enough to restrict a person's lifestyle.

Basic vapours

Congestion of the airways can be treated by inhaling various volatile substances (see glossary) such as oils, resins and camphor. In a traditional treatment, a small amount of the substance is put into a bowl of very hot water and the fumes inhaled under a towel draped over the head and the bowl. Alternatively, an ointment containing the volatile substance is rubbed onto the chest, so that its fumes can be steadily inhaled. Many people still use plastic "inhalers" — a tube with a small amount of oil inside — to clear a stuffed-up nose.

Breathing anaesthetic

During an operation, the patient is given an anaesthetic so that he or she becomes unconscious and does not feel pain. A mixture of gases including oxygen is bubbled through a volatile liquid anaesthetic and given to the patient through a face mask and a tube inserted down the windpipe.

The mixture is carefully regulated by an anaesthetist so that the patient gets enough oxygen to maintain the body's vital functions whilst he or she is unconscious and keep the tissues alive. Immediately after the operation and during recovery, extra oxygen may be given to help to bring the patient back to consciousness.

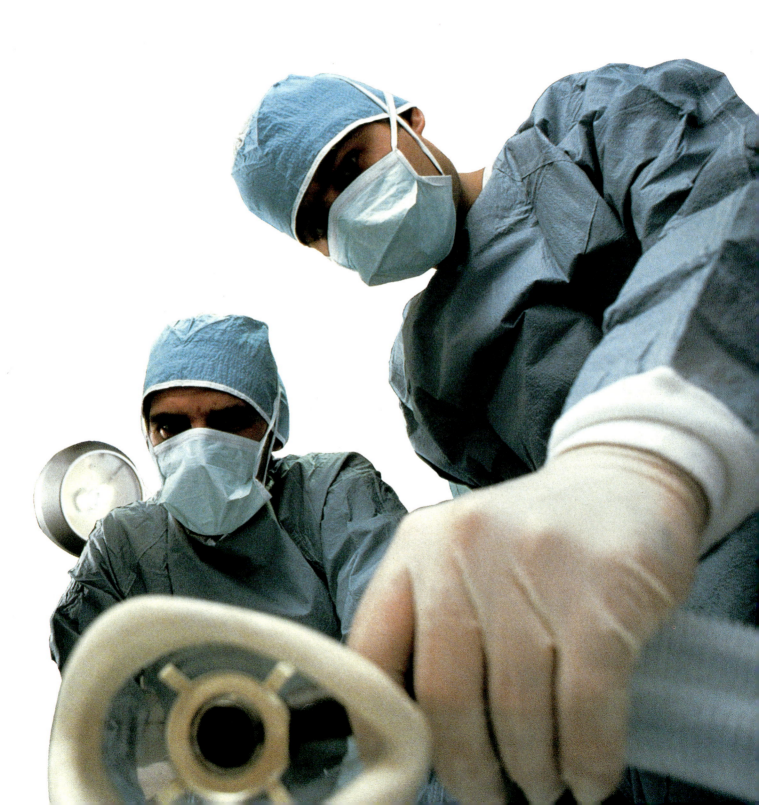

16 WHY DO PEOPLE SNIFF?

There is nothing special about sniffing solvents. People sniff for more or less the same reasons that other people smoke, drink, or take illegal drugs such as crack or heroin. No two people are the same and everybody who sniffs has his or her own personal reasons. Most young people do it because it happens to be the fashion at their school at the time. Some of their friends do it, so they do as well. Teenagers like to do things that would shock their parents and teachers. They may smoke, have their hair cut in strange ways or wear way-out clothes. Others may sniff solvents. Sniffing can be exciting for a while, if the rest of the world seems dull and boring. However, some people sniff by themselves. Usually these are the ones with serious problems at home, school or work.

Domestic problems

For some young people, home is not a nice place to be. If mother or father is out of work, there will not be much money coming in. The house may be uncomfortable, cold and damp.

The family may be hungry and there might be arguing day and night. Mother or father may drink too much. There could be violence in the house. Anybody in this situation might want to escape the problems, and sniffing solvents might seem one way to do this.

The loner

The person who sniffs alone is usually the one with the most problems. Sometimes trouble at home or school leads people to try sniffing. People in trouble who feel they have nobody to talk to often want to escape. But if they are young, they might not have anywhere to run to. So they might try running away inside their heads. To escape like this, somebody might drink, take drugs or sniff solvents. Usually lone sniffers start because all their friends are doing it. But the problems do not go away, and they do it more and more often. So they sniff by themselves.

Peer pressure

Young people do lots of things simply because their friends do them. Nobody wants to feel left out. Everyone likes to feel they are part of the group. Even if the person doesn't really want to do something, they feel under pressure to be like their friends or "the gang".

Being pushed into doing things by friends is called "peer pressure". Somebody might feel obliged to "sniff", smoke, draw graffitti on the wall, or play truant from school.

18 WHY DO PEOPLE SNIFF?

Easily hidden

Products containing solvents, substances that can be inhaled, are everywhere. Nobody would take much notice of a school child using glue to stick paper together, using modelling cement to build a construction kit, or drawing with a magic marker. Many products are in small tubes or packets. Some solvents can be used without anybody seeing. Glue can be rubbed into sleeves or jacket lapels and sniffed. People who smoke might also be sniffing the lighter fuel they use to light their cigarettes.

A question of money

It is usually young people who sniff inhalants. Why? Mainly because it is the cheapest way of changing how you feel. Illegal drugs cost a lot of money. They are also quite difficult to get hold of. Alcohol is easier to buy, but in Britain you cannot legally buy it at a supermarket or in a pub until you are over 18 years old.

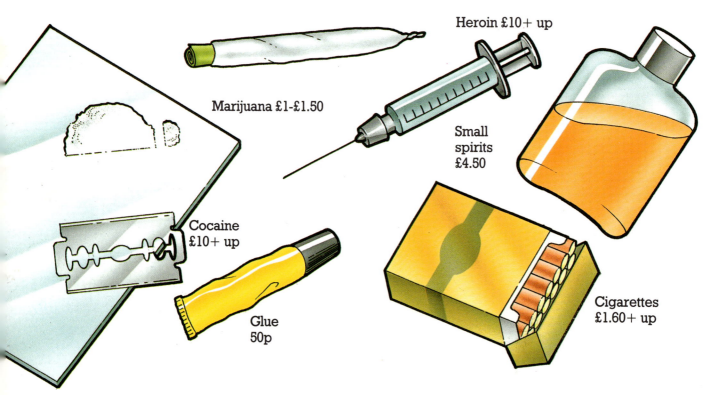

Fast effects

We live in a "fast" society. Nobody wants to wait for anything. We have fast food, we have remote controls for TV and video. Computers that do not respond immediately are regarded as rubbish. The same applies to the effects of drugs and inhalants. Users want something to happen now! When they are sniffed or inhaled, solvent vapours are absorbed through the lungs. From there vapours go into the blood and straight to the brain. This is why the effects of solvents are felt quickly. And this is what a lot of sniffers think that they want.

Shock-value

Newspapers have been full of scare stories about the dangers of sniffing solvents. Some teenagers like to shock their parents by doing dangerous things. But they do not actually want to hurt themselves. They just want to "act big" in front of their friends. However, some young people with lots of personal problems are so unhappy that they do not really care what happens to themselves. In the long run, sniffing inhalants will not make depression and boredom go away.

20 WHAT IS THE EFFECT?

Sniffing inhalants is a bit like getting drunk. The sniffer feels light-headed, dizzy and happy. Giggling fits are common. Speech is slurred and the sniffer may see double. It might be difficult to stand up properly. First-time users often just feel sick and drowsy. This puts off many people from doing it again. Like alcohol, what happens depends on how the sniffer feels before he or she starts, who they are with, and so on. For instance, the experience of sniffing is likely to be bad if you are feeling depressed anyway, or if you are sniffing in a strange place, or with people you do not know very well. Many sniffers report having hallucinations – seeing things that are not there – like snakes or spiders. These effects happen almost straight away and can last up to half an hour.

No inhibitions

One effect of sniffing inhalants is to reduce inhibitions – that is, to make people very relaxed and perhaps to forget rules of correct behaviour. They may then do things that they would not do if unaffected by inhalants, things they may well regret later.

Loss of balance

Inhalants can interfere with the sense of balance and make you feel giddy. In high doses they can even give the sensation of floating in the air. You lose your balance and cannot walk straight but stumble along. You may even fall over and be unable to stand up again. Some people feel sick – rather like being sea-sick – and may vomit. All in all the effects of sniffing inhalants are to upset the mind's mental balance as well as the body's physical balance. Sniffers tend to stumble along, fall over, look silly and sit down laughing at each other.

Hallucinations

Sniffers often say they see things when they use inhalants. These can be cartoon monsters, shooting stars, trees that move, and so on. These are called hallucinations. A group of sniffers may even see the same hallucination. The people who see them know in their minds that they are not real.

WHAT ARE THE EFFECTS?

Intoxication

Many inhalants act like alcohol does and cause intoxication. Alcohol and inhalants are poisons which interfere with the working of the brain. The first effect is usually to slow down reactions. People lose their inhibitions and become "happy" or silly, although in an argument they are much more likely to become aggressive. The next sign of continuing intoxication is unsteadiness on the feet and clumsiness – people knock things over and have difficulty standing up straight.

Speech may become slurred; nausea and vomiting may follow. The final stage is unconsciousness. There are two main dangers of intoxication. While people are confused, they may easily injure themselves or cause injury to others. They may get into a fight or become involved in a road accident. The second danger is that they may be sick while unconscious and choke on the vomit.

Aggression

Some people get violent when they have had too much to drink. The same can happen with inhalants. Often gangs who are quite aggressive anyway become more so after a sniffing session. They may have been drinking as well. However, the newspapers tend to blame everything that vandals do on solvent sniffing. This is often not really the case. What is certain, however, is that inhalant users get disorientated and confused. They can suddenly shift from having fun to wanting a fight.

Enough is enough

One effect of solvents is to reduce the amount of oxygen in the blood. A person's breathing and heartbeat slow down. If a person keeps on sniffing or if he or she inhales very deeply, there is the danger of an "overdose". They might feel confused and unable to control their movements.

They may fall unconscious. First-time users might feel very ill and sick. But usually no harm is done if they soon stop.

24 IMMEDIATE DANGERS

The immediate dangers of sniffing inhalants fall into four main groups. The first is accidents. There is always the chance of an accident if somebody is "drunk" on inhalants. They may injure themselves or other people. Second, is the way inhalants are sniffed. Some people use large plastic bags to sniff glue. If you fall asleep, or lose consciousness, with a plastic bag on your head you might well suffocate. Third is that some inhalants are more dangerous than others. The most dangerous are aerosol cans. Spraying aerosol straight into the lungs reduces the amount of oxygen in the blood. If you do not have enough oxygen you might die. This leads to the fourth main danger – death. For a few unlucky people, the first time they sniffed inhalants was the last time. The dangers aren't worth the risk.

Sniffer's rash

People who sniff glue often get a reddening of the skin around the mouth and on the lips. There may be lots of small spots or pimples, resembling acne. This condition is known as sniffer's rash, and it is caused by repeatedly putting a plastic bag to the mouth.

Tolerance

After people have been sniffing inhalants regularly for a while, they need to sniff more and more to get the same effects. They also have to sniff more often. This is called tolerance, and is one of the first steps towards physical dependence, or addiction.

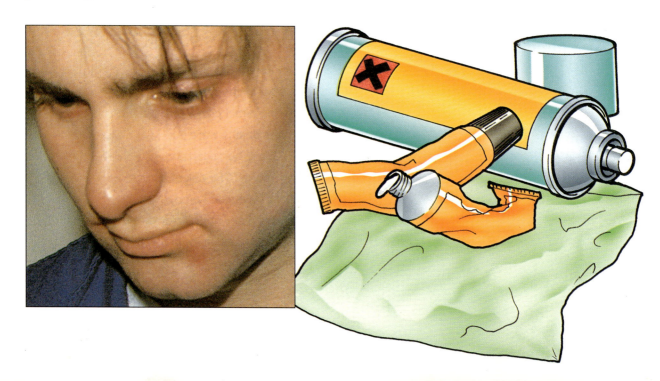

Accidents

Accidents with solvent sniffing can happen in a number of ways. People who sniff do not want to be seen by their parents or the police. So they may hide away in an old building with holes in the floor, or near a canal, or under a bridge or on a railway line.

If they lose control over what they are doing, they may for instance, fall into the canal. It is also very dangerous to sniff and then work machinery or ride a bike or drive a car. Some people may hide and sniff in a very small space, such as a closet. They could easily be overcome by the fumes and fall unconscious. Those who sniff lighter fuel could set fire to themselves if cigarettes are being smoked as well. Finally somebody could suffocate by sniffing glue or another inhalant from a large plastic bag.

Sudden death

There is always the risk of death from sniffing inhalants. Sometimes it happens because the person suffocates on a plastic bag. Sometimes it happens because the person chokes on vomit while unconscious. Sometimes it happens because he or she is inhaling a particularly dangerous solvent. All aerosols are dangerous. So is lighter fuel and typewriter fluid. These inhalants can cause the heart and the lungs to stop working.

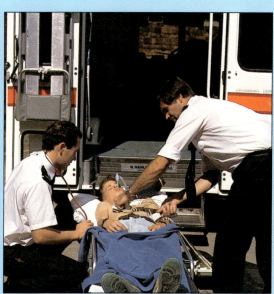

LONG-TERM DANGERS

There are a number of problems which may occur for people who have been sniffing for a long time, that is for a few years. They will probably have a rash around their mouth, which can be one way of telling if somebody is sniffing solvents. Some may have to sniff more and more in order to get the same effects. They may also feel very ill if they try to stop. Somebody who has a problem with their nervous system might make it worse by sniffing. Sniffing aerosols and cleaning fluid may well cause liver and kidney damage. But what usually happens is that most problems with inhalants go away once the person has stopped. Many people who sniff do not suffer any long-term damage, even those who have been sniffing for a long time. However, there are deaths every year due to sniffing.

Loss of appetite

People who sniff for a long time are usually very unhappy. Feeling bad about yourself and your world is one reason why people sniff solvents in the first place. Somebody feeling like this may not take very good care of themselves.

If they do not eat properly inhalants will make things worse. They affect the appetite and people's health often goes downhill as a result. Sniffers easily catch coughs, colds and the flu.

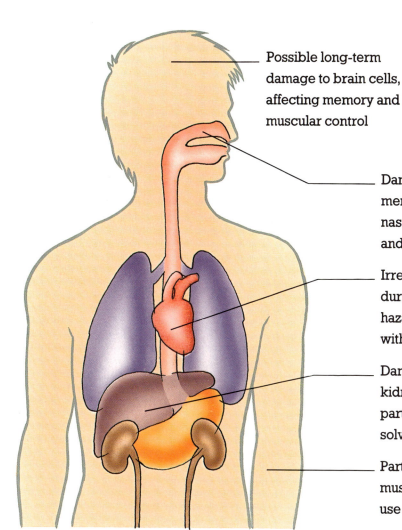

- Possible long-term damage to brain cells, affecting memory and muscular control
- Psychological dependence, in which sniffing is thought to solve personal problems
- Damage to the mucous membranes lining the nasal passages, throat and airways to the lungs
- Irregular heartbeat during sniffing, hazardous to somebody with a heart disorder
- Damage to the liver and kidneys, caused particularly by inhaling solvents
- Partial paralysis of muscles from long-term use of inhalants

More severe effects

The more severe effects from sniffing inhalants are very rare – but they do happen. Sniffing for years may mean some loss of control over body movements. This shows that there is brain damage. The liver and kidneys can be damaged by sniffing aerosols and cleaning fluids. These problems do not go away even if the person stops. The lead in petrol can also cause brain damage if sniffed over a period of time. While somebody is sniffing, the heart beat can be affected. This can be extremely dangerous over a time for somebody who already has a heart problem, especially if he or she do not know about it.

Dependence

Some sniffers get headaches when they stop sniffing. It is often a sign of physical dependence. A few people with lots of problems may feel they need to sniff a lot of the time. They think it helps them cope with their problems. This is called psychological dependence.

28 INHALANTS IN SOCIETY

Society itself can be partly to blame for somebody becoming a heavy sniffer. For example, there may be problems at home because parents are out of work and there is little money to spend. But people who are sniffing a lot can in turn cause problems. Their parents may be very worried. They may start missing school. They may steal inhalants from shops. They can get into trouble with the police. Other people might have to get involved to sort the problems out. These might be a doctor, a social worker or perhaps a psychiatrist. Imagine a stone landing in a pond. There are ripples that spread out right across the pond from where the stone falls. The stone is the sniffer. The pond is society. And the ripples are all the effects of sniffing reaching far and wide.

Pressure on family

An inhalant-sniffing problem in the family is a problem for everybody. Parents will wonder why it has happened. How can they stop it? Where can they go for help? Money may be stolen to pay for inhalants. The sniffer might be playing truant. There could be a visits from the police. The family may get the blame for what has happened.

Vandalism

Many inhalant users do not seem to be interested in simply getting "high". They are really after something exciting and dangerous. They find fun in doing things which other people disapprove of. They know that their actions will shock parents, teachers or those in authority. Such sniffers often turn to vandalism while under the influence of an inhalant. By defacing a wall, or breaking something in public, they can be sure to get the reaction they are after.

Crime

Sniffers often steal money from home or school to pay for inhalants. They often steal from shops. A gang of sniffers may damage property because the effect of the inhalant makes them feel brave, in much the same way that alcohol might. Personal problems can get worse if there is trouble with the police.

THE LAW

There is no law against sniffing inhalants. There is no law against having inhalants. But a sniffer may get into trouble because of what he or she does when under the influence of solvents. Also shopkeepers may be breaking the law if they sell inhalants to somebody under the age of 18.

Sniffing solvents is not illegal. But if a group of sniffers is being rude or noisy on the streets, they could be charged with "a breach of the peace". It is not illegal to buy inhalants. But if the shopkeeper sells inhalants to somebody under 18 and knows (or has a good idea) that the solvents will be sniffed – then the law has been broken. Driving a car while under the influence of inhalants is illegal. It is the same as driving when you have had too much to drink.

The laws in Scotland are a bit different. In Scotland, somebody who is caught sniffing may be investigated by a Children's Panel. This Panel can put somebody into care if the sniffing is the result of problems in the family. There is also a law in Scotland which bans the sale of solvents to anybody who might misuse them. Some politicians think there should be a law so that the makers of solvents would have to put very unpleasant smells in them.

GLOSSARY

airways passages that lead air to and from the lungs, including the trachea (windpipe) and bronchi.

allergy over-reaction to the presence of foreign substances in contact with the body, and to certain foods and medicines.

asthma usually allergic reaction that causes the airways to constrict (become narrow), resulting in difficulty in breathing.

bronchodilator drug used in anti-asthma sprays.

evaporation process by which a liquid changes to a gas or vapour. Liquid that evaporates rapidly at ordinary temperatures is called volatile; most solvents are volatile.

inhalant any substance that can be sniffed or breathed in.

propellant gas gas under pressure in an aerosol spray, used to push out the substance being sprayed.

solvent liquid used for its ability to dissolve substances, for instance in paints, varnishes and dry-cleaning fluids. Most solvents are volatile and evaporate quickly.

tolerance ability of the body to deal with the effects of a drug. High tolerance is a symptom of dependence (addiction).

vapour state of matter in which it exists as a gas; warming a liquid makes it turn into a vapour.

volatile *see* evaporation.

ADDRESSES FOR HELP AND INFORMATION

Institute for the Study of Drug Dependence
1 Hatton Place
London EC1N 8ND.
Tel: 01-430 1993.

For additional information about solvent misuse – booklets, leaflets, reading list, etc.

The Society for the Prevention of Solvent and Volatile Substance Abuse
St Mary's Chambers
19 Station Road, Stone
Staffordshire ST15 8JP.
Tel: 0785 817885/46097.

Produces information sheets, booklets, videos etc. on solvent misuse. Also can assist in finding help for solvent misusers and their families in their area.

National Campaign Against Solvent Abuse
Box 513
245a Coldharbour Lane
London SW9 8RR.
Tel: 01-274-7700 (office).
Tel: 01-733-7330 (helpline).

Help and advice for solvent misusers and their families.

INDEX

accident 24, 25
addiction 24, 27
adhesive 8-9
aerosol 7, 8-9, 10-11
alcohol 22
ammonia 12-13
amyl nitrate 12-13
anaesthetic 10-11, 14-15
angina 12-13
appetite 26
asthma 12-13, 14-15

benzene 10-11
brain damage 27
bronchitis 12-13
bronchocilator 12-13

cleaning agent 8-9, 10-11

dangers 24-27
death 24, 25, 29
dependence 27

effects 19, 20
electroplating 8-9
ether 5, 10-11

glue 7, 8-9

hallucinations 20
hay fever 14
heart disease 12-13

inhibitions 20
intoxication 22

kerosene 10-11

laughing gas 10-11
law 30

medical inhalants 12-13

nasal spray 14-15
Nations Campaign Against Solvent Abuse 31
nitrous oxide 10-11

overdose 23
oxygen 12-13, 14-15

paint 7, 8-9
paraffin 10-11
peer pressure 17
propellant 7

recovery position 25
rotahaler 12

smelling salts 13
sniffer's rash 24
sniffing 16
Society for the Prevention of Solvent and Volatile Substance Abuse 31
solvent 6, 8-9
suffocation 24, 25

tolerance 24

vapour 6
volatile hyorocarbon 6